Girls

On the Street

Girls

On the Street

by

Rumbidzai Rurevo and Michael Bourdillon

WEAVER
W
—PRESS—

Published by
Weaver Press
Box A1922, Avondale
Harare, Zimbabwe

© Rumbidzai Rurevo and Michael Bourdillon, 2003

The authors and the publisher would like to express their thanks
to Save the Children (Norway) and to Street Child Africa (Thames
Ditton, UK) for their generous support of this publication.

Typeset by Fontline Electronic Publishing, Harare, Zimbabwe.
Cover designed by Danes Design, Harare
Printed and bound in Zimbabwe by Bardwell Printers

ISBN: 1 77922 016 2

🕭 Acknowledgements ✍

We wish to thank first of all the girls who gave freely of their time to help Rumbidzai Rurevo with this study. We hope that an improved understanding of their plight will, in the long term, improve their lives and those of other girls who find themselves on the streets. We owe our thanks also to concerned adults for their co-operation and patience, particularly to the staff of Streets Ahead

We are grateful to Linda Dube for his help in planning and conducting the research, and commenting on early drafts of the report

The publication of this material would not have been possible without the support of Save the Children, Norway, to whom we are grateful. We thank Lois Mushonga for her encouragement and support, and Caroline Chikowore and Shumba Sibongile for useful comments on an early draft of the document.

Elisabeth Lickindorf gave much time freely to help us improve the text, and we offer our thanks.

🐦 The authors 🐦

Rumbidzai Rurevo did this research as part of her M.Sc. degree in Sociology at the University of Zimbabwe. She now works in the civil service in Harare.

Professor Michael Bourdillon has taught in the Department of Sociology, University of Zimbabwe, for over 25 years, and for over ten years has been involved in an organisation dedicated to helping street children. His recent publications include: *Where are the Ancestors? Changing culture in Zimbabwe*; *Earning a Life: Working Children in Zimbabwe*; and *Women, Men and Work: Rural livelihoods in south-eastern Zimbabwe*.

✍ Contents ✍

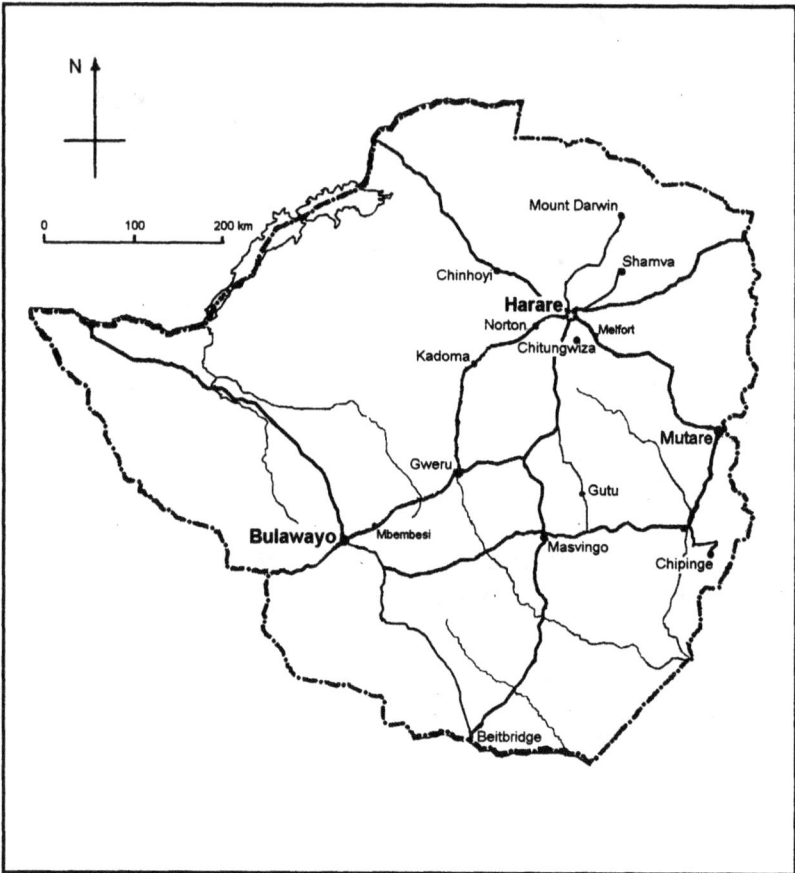

Map 1: Zimbabwe

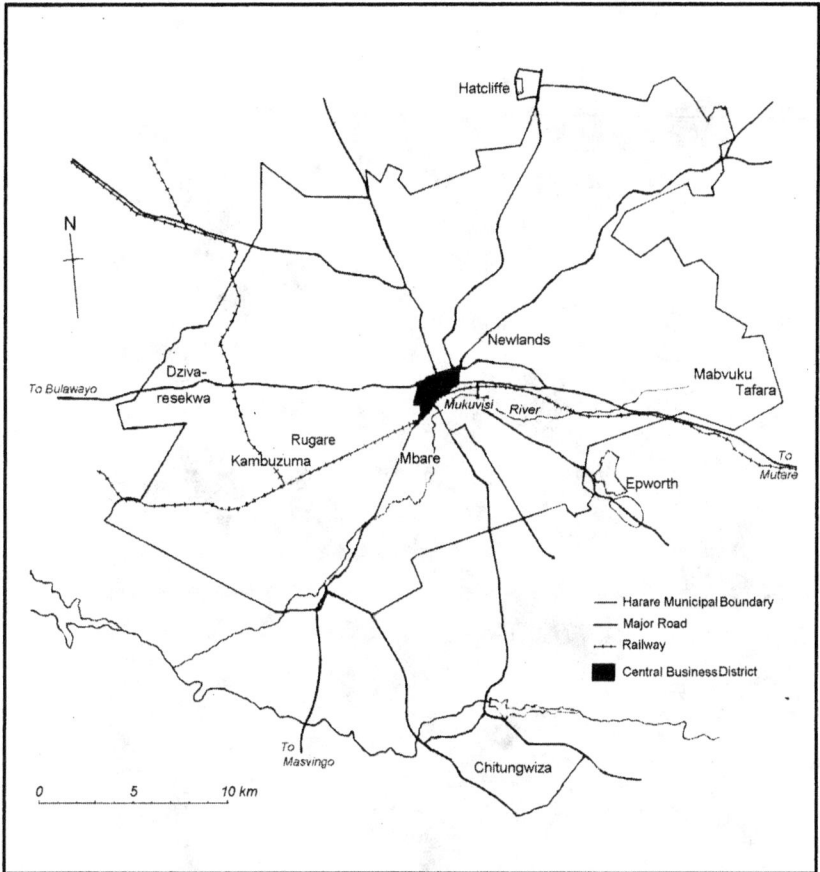

Map 2: Harare

Photograph by Tsvangirayi Mukwazhi

🐾 Background 🐾

Rumbidzai Rurevo and Michael Bourdillon

Introduction

Shocking information emerged from Rumbidzai Rurevo's study of street girls from December 2000 to February 2001.[1] We believe it needs to be available to a wider audience, in the hope that people will change their attitudes to these deprived children and do what they can to help them. Although limited in scope, this study of the life experiences of street girls exposes their serious plight, and society's need to take their problems seriously.

Girls in the streets have been sidelined and overlooked both physically and in research.[2] Although people in Harare accept that girls may accompany blind or disabled parents on the streets, the street is normally seen as a domain for boys. Girls who have dared to venture into them and live there independently like boys have been stigmatised as prostitutes. Some girls appear sporadically

---

[1] The central chapter of this book is Rumbidzai Rurevo's report of her findings. The two authors together wrote the first and last chapters.

[2] See Barbara Lopi and Merab K. Kiremire, *Invisible Girls: The Life Circumstances and Legal Situation of Street Girls in Lusaka*. Zambia Association for Research and Development and Movement of Community Action for the Prevention and Protection of Young People against Poverty, Destitution, Diseases and Exploitation, Lusaka, 2001: 5.

on the streets, looking well dressed and well nourished, and are hardly noticed as in need of care. But opportunities for girls to make a living on the streets are extremely limited, and our stories indicate that virtually all of them use sex at some time to sustain their lives. In the current context of an AIDS epidemic, this sustenance is very short-term. The plight of girls on the streets is desperately dangerous.

Street children

Street children became an issue during the International Year of the Child in 1979, which marked the beginning of the growing global concern for the welfare of children and anxiety about the increasing numbers of street children.[3] The last two decades have marked the extension of human rights to encapsulate the rights of the child, culminating in the United Nations Convention on the Rights of the Child, which was written over ten years, from 1979-1989, and adopted by the General Assembly of the United Nations in 1989. It is a widely ratified instrument in the history of mankind, with only the United States and Somalia not having endorsed the spirit and provisions of this document. Many governments and non-governmental organisations have increased their activities to alleviate the plight of street children.

In Zimbabwe, street children appear to be a relatively recent phenomenon. In the colonial era, it was impossible for children to work in the street as municipal by-laws that restricted this were strictly and brutally enforced.[4] Independence in 1980 saw a relaxation in the enforcement of municipal influx control laws, and the urban

---

[3] For a general account, see S. Agnelli, *Street Children: A Growing Urban Tragedy*. Weidenfeld and Nicholson, London, 1986. More recently A. Butcher, *Street Children*, Nelson Word Publishing, Nashville (TN), 1996. Also Lewis Aptekar 'Street Children in the Developing World: A Review of their Condition' in *Cross Cultural Research* 28 (1994), 3: 195-224.

[4] See Beverly Grier, 'Street kids in Zimbabwe: The historical origins of a contemporary problem,' a paper presented at the Annual Meeting of the African Studies Association, November 25, 1996, San Francisco, CA, USA.

population swelled dramatically, straining housing and other social facilities. By the 1990s, the economy could not create sufficient jobs, which resulted in a growing informal sector: by the end of the century unemployment had dramatically increased.[5]

Numbers of street children are hard to assess with any accuracy. A survey in Harare towards the end of the year 2000 estimated that there were around 5 000 children on the streets of the city. The numbers have been increasing with growing unemployment and poverty. Many of these children spend much of their time on the streets of the city, where they obtain their livelihood, but have a home of some kind to go to at night. At the end of 2002, Streets Ahead, an organisation focussing on children living on the streets, had around 1 500 children on its books, of whom just over 200 were girls. These are children who at some stage have sought or accepted help from the organisation. As we shall see, some children avoid the intervention of such organisations, so the figures that are available are far from comprehensive. Nevertheless, they indicate the magnitude of the problem.

The phenomenon of street children emerged in the urban landscape of Zimbabwe in the late 1980s, especially in the capital city, Harare. They were considered a blemish on the city and a problem that needed an urgent solution. Increasingly, residents and visitors complained of being accosted by little children accompanying adults begging for money. Motorists disliked being harassed by youths who 'own' parking bays. People objected to having to pay fees to have their cars parked and guarded, whether or not they wanted this service.

---

[5] We do not have accurate figures for unemployment in Zimbabwe, but the following gives an indication of the scale of the problem. In 1990, when the population of the country was around 9,7 million, there were 1,229 million (12,7 percent) in formal employment. In 2000, when the population was around 12,5 million, there were 1,231 million (9,8 percent) in formal employment. (See Central Statistical Office, Harare, *Quarterly Digest of Statistics*, September 1991, table 5, and September 2002, table 6. Populations are estimated from the 1992 Census and the 1997 Inter-Census Survey.)

Migration from rural areas to towns has fuelled growth in urbanisation, which is not matched by industrialisation or job creation. The collapse of the Zimbabwean economy in the late 1990s has resulted in large-scale unemployment and urban poverty. Schooling has become more expensive, and is not valued as a guarantor of future employment. At the same time, movements of people have weakened traditional extended family and community ties, as families become separated and have to fend for themselves. The adverse effects of these changes have included the break down of family values and the traditional systems of care by the extended family and community.[6]

Another serious factor is the helplessness of those affected by HIV/AIDS. Even uninfected children suffer, as household incomes are lost when sick parents are no longer able to work and have to spend their savings on treatment. When the parents die, children may have no one to look after them, or inadequate care, and find their way onto the streets. One estimate is that there are over a million orphans in Zimbabwe.[7] In a study of street children in Harare, about a third said that one or both of their parents were dead.[8]

Socio-cultural factors, including traditional perceptions of childhood and the roles of children by gender, might also play a critical part in determining who amongst siblings should work to support the family. Some children are perceived as an economic burden rather than an investment and are forced out of school to earn money. This is particularly true of girls. Out of school, they

---

[6]   See M.F.C. Bourdillon, *Where are the Ancestors? Changing Culture in Zimbabwe*. University of Zimbabwe Press, Harare, 1997 (2nd ed.): 19-34. For a similar phenomenon facing street children in South America, see J. Swart, 'Street children in Latin America with special reference to Guatemala' *Unisa Latin America Report* G (1), Pretoria, March 1990 (28-42).

[7]   UNICEF, *Zimbabwe Progress Report*. UNICEF, Harare, 1999.

[8]   Yotamu Chirwa and Markim Wakatama, 'Working Street Children in Harare' in *Earning a Life: working children in Zimbabwe* (ed.) Michael Bourdillon. Weaver Press, Harare, 2000, p.47.

have to undertake domestic duties, and work in the informal sector if possible. To fulfil traditional obligations in a crisis, children might work to settle family debts, pay medical fees or to contribute to their own education or that of siblings.

In the past, girls were more protected than were boys within the same family, to the extent that girls would not take to the streets easily and few were to be seen there.[9] Those who did find their way onto the streets were quickly taken up by 'aunties', who would give them a home and clothes in exchange for their services as prostitutes. Boys in Harare complained that the girls they had once mixed with would soon consider themselves above the class of the boys.[10] Because boys were more prominent on the streets, early programmes for street children focussed on boys to the neglect of girls.[11]

As more families are sucked into poverty and income from children becomes more important for the livelihood of such families, protection has diminished and girls are finding their way onto the streets in greater numbers. We find a common pattern. A woman, often without male support, ekes out a meagre living from informal trading on the streets; her daughter helps with the stall and the sale of wares. Such girls easily move into their own informal enterprises, often following their mothers in supplementing their income through the trade of sex.[12]

Some children end up on the streets because the adults who should care for them instead abandon, abuse, or neglect them. A

---

[9]   The country-wide survey by B. Muchini and S. Nyandiya-Bundy estimated only 5 per cent children on the streets were girls. 'Struggling to survive; a study of Street Children in Zimbabwe', Department of Psychology, University of Zimbabwe, and UNICEF, Harare, 1991.

[10] M.F.C. Bourdillon, 'Street children in Harare'. *Africa* 64 (1994), 4: 518-19.

[11] See, for example, L. Dube, L. Kamvura, and M.F.C. Bourdillon, 'Working with street boys in Harare.' *Africa Insight* 26 (1996), 3: 260-67.

[12] For examples of this practice, see Virginia Mapedzahama and Michael Bourdillon, 'Street workers in a Harare suburb'; Martha Mutisi and Michael Bourdillon 'Child vendors at a rural growth point'. In *Earning a Life; working children in Zimbabwe*, Michael Bourdillon (ed.), Weaver Press, Harare, 2000. 25-44; 75-94.

girl might be sent to a relative to help with housework and especially to care for a sick relation, and in some cases the children are unwilling partners in the arrangement, or perceive they are not being treated fairly. In extreme cases, girls can be pledged to other families to meet traditional obligations to appease an angry spirit (*ngozi*) or to obtain help in a crisis. They might find their situation intolerable and flee to the streets.

Individual factors are also important. One child in a family of six children, for instance, might take to the streets while the other five remain at home. Thus, issues of tolerance to stress and personal disposition of each individual child are said to be important in determining which amongst siblings takes to the streets. 'It is a matter as much of character and biology (that is of personality) as it is of fate and environment.'[13]

Treatment and perceptions

People in power often perceive street children to be criminals (or at least potential criminals), and in any case a slur on the city. Consequently, they take a punitive approach towards street children, forcefully removing them from the streets and placing them in detention centres for children, often technically referred to as 'houses of safety'.[14] In some countries, the forceful removal of street children results in physical harm, or even in death.[15] The motive for such action is public safety and well being, rather than the well being of the children. Inadequate provisions made for children in law lead to violent episodic removal of street children, and this generally results in the state machinery infringing on the rights of the children. Public officials take the punitive stance partly as a result of pressure

---

[13] J.K. Felsman 'Abandoned children: a reconsideration', *Children Today*, May-June, 1984: 13.

[14] M.F.C. Bourdillon, 'Street children in Harare'. 526-7. L. Dube, Street Children: a part of organised society? Unpublished D.Phil. Dissertation, University of Zimbabwe, Harare, 1999.

[15] A. Vittachi, *Stolen Childhood: In Search of the Rights of the Child*. Polity Press, Cambridge, 1989: 7.

from officials in industry and commerce in the city centre, who feel that street children drive away potential business.[16]

Adults often take for granted that they know better than children. They often seek to solve the problems of children without reference to the children's views and perspectives. They easily forget that children are persons, with their own experience and knowledge, leading to their individual feelings, preferences and choices about their lives. As persons, children have a right that their knowledge and preferences concerning their lives be taken seriously. Furthermore, organisations striving to provide for the needs of children – adequate shelter, food, protection, education and adult care – emphasise children's dependence on adults. The potential competence of children is connected to stages in development towards adulthood. Children are deemed to be incompetent in an adult sphere and to be in need of protection against abuse. This paradigm often conceals children's competence within their own spheres of interaction, particularly their ability to work out survival and coping strategies on the streets.[17] It also arises from and supports the assumption that the family is the normal social and biological structure within which the child should grow, and pays insufficient attention to other contexts in which a child can develop.

Following this paradigm, attempts at intervention usually involve taking the children off the streets as quickly as possible, rounding them up, placing them in institutions where there are no alternatives, and rehabilitating them with education and skills programmes. Our study coincided with a series of round-ups of street children over

---

[16] See with reference to South Africa J. Swart-Kruger 'An imperfect fit – street children and state intervention'. *Africa Insight* 26, 3: 236. On the general perception of street children in terms of society's problems rather than the children's see B. Glauser, 'Street Children: Deconstructing a Construct' in James, A. & Prout, A. (eds) *Constructing and Reconstructing Childhood: Contemporary Issues in the Sociological Study of Childhood* , The Falmer Press: London, 1990, 136-56.

[17] See Rachel Baker, 1998 'Runaway street children in Nepal: social competence away from home', (p.51) in *Children and Social Competence: Areas of Action* (ed.) Ian Hutchby, and Jo Moran-Ellis. Falmer Press, London, 1998, 51.

four months (from November 2000 to February 2001). In such exercises, children are forcefully taken off the streets and to a centre where authorities from the Department of Social Welfare interview them and, where they think appropriate, commit them to institutions. The official reason for such action is to protect the children from abuse, particularly sexual abuse, and from negligent parents. The children try to escape this 'protection' and claim that such policies cannot work, because those committed to institutions soon manage to abscond from them.[18]

Apart from the practical problems of such an approach is the conceptual problem that it is based on a globalised paradigm of childhood, or perhaps middle-class perceptions of what childhood should be. It pays insufficient attention to particular local circumstances and the situation of the children, and it ignores the status that children gain in poor families from their contributions to the family livelihood.

Public reaction to street children often reflects the view that children are competent only for learning and play, under the control and care of adults. When some children do not fit this paradigm, others become uncomfortable, and readily judge the children and their situation as anti-social. Where children work for an income, even if it is for the benefit of their families, child labour is condemned.[19] Poor and desperate children appearing on the streets spoil the illusion that our city is managed well, and the children are blamed. People frequently refer to street children as urchins and thieves, and often violent, paying little attention to their personal circumstances or to the motives that drive them onto the streets.

Girl children on the streets are particularly stigmatised. They are perceived to be prostitutes, not worthy of being properly

---

[18] See report in *The Herald*, October 3, 2000: 'Scores of street kids rounded up'.

[19] For a discussion of perceptions of child labour in Zimbabwe, see Michael Bourdillon (ed.) *Earning a Life: working children in Zimbabwe*, Weaver Press, Harare, 2000, 'Introduction', 1-24.

maintained as a sexual partner. During the study, Rurevo frequently heard derogatory remarks about the children with whom she was spending her time:

These are not street children...

These girls are just lazy and unemployable. They do not want to work. They would rather have easy money. Nothing good comes from the streets.

Most girls from poor families are working as domestic maids[20] so why should they just come and sit in the streets?

Opinions differ as to whether street children should be assisted on the streets or removed to another place. Feeding children within the street environments is said to attract and encourage more children onto the street. Over the years, episodic removal of children from the streets has not proved a solution. Some children return to the streets and others are initiated into street life, as the factors that continue to drive them onto the streets remain. The institutionalisation of street children has not yielded the desired results of persuading children to revert to childhood activities like schooling and playing,[21] as street children have in the meantime developed different ideas of what childhood is about.

Another paradigm takes into account children's liberation from adult dominance, and recognises children as capable of responding to situations of adversity.[22] To achieve better results when working

---

[20] It is a common practice for girls from poor families to be provided with food and accommodation in exchange for domestic services. The services are often unpaid and usually undefined, meaning that the girl is on call all day and night, every day.

[21] While middle-class people in Zimbabwe readily iterate the middle-class Western idea that childhood is about school and play, playing receives little attention as a means of childhood development.

[22] Judith Ennew, *Street and working children: A guide to planning*. Save the Children, London, 1994, 201. For changes in emphasis in studies of street children in Brazil, see Udi Butler and Irene Rizzini, 'Young people living and working on the streets of Brazil: revisiting the literature', *International Journal of Educational Policy, Research and Practice* (University of South Florida, USA), 2 (2001), 4.

with street children, adults need to learn about, and bolster, street children's areas of competence. This approach begins with respect for the dignity of the children, for the contributions they make to their families and communities, and for their right and capacity to shape their own lives. It protects the children in their locations and their occupations, and improves their skills for work in their chosen environment. It treats all children with full respect for their rights, opinions, potential and individuality.[23]

In line with this paradigm, research on street children should look at the advantages and disadvantages of street life from the point of view of the children. It follows that legislative policy planning for street children should be sensitive to the reasons why they work and live in the streets; children themselves should be allowed to participate, to ensure that legal action is based on familiarity with their lives and thus enhance the likelihood of its success. This paradigm accords with current thinking on children's rights, and especially the right of children to have a say in decisions that affect them. On the other hand, the AIDS epidemic makes life on the streets lethal. Recently a group of around 30 children from the streets of Harare were tested for the HIV virus: only two boys were free of it.

Those girls who choose to live on the streets independently for various reasons have shown that, like their boy counterparts, they manage within networks that provide some protection, despite the fact that they are highly susceptible to exploitation, especially sexual exploitation. The girls, like the boys, are capable of independent living and exhibit competencies in pursuit of independent life on the streets. Yet, as this study shows, their situation is so perilous that it is not clear how they can best be helped.

---

[23]   See, for example, W.E. Myers, and Jo Boyden, *Child labour; Promoting the best interests of working children.* Save the Children, London, 1998, 8.

Intervention Programmes

A number of organisations and programmes currently operating in Harare have been of some service to the street girls we met. Here, we briefly introduce the programmes mentioned in the accounts of the children that follow.

Streets Ahead is a non-governmental organisation that is largely donor-funded, and dedicated to helping destitute children to become spiritually, physically and financially self-sufficient. Established in 1991, the organisation mainly works with street children and other underprivileged children away from home. At the time of our study, it operated a drop-in centre, which provided the children with washing, cooking and recreational facilities, and a base for educational and training programmes.

The organisation is unique in employing a small team of outreach workers to visit the children on the streets. The aim is to get the children off the streets, preferably reunited with their families. But no compulsion is used. The outreach workers also help children to access services such as medical care and sometimes even social welfare.

A volunteer working with girls at Streets Ahead.

Photograph courtesy of Streets Ahead

The organisation runs a 'street peer' programme, in which, under guidance from the staff, certain older children are elected by other children to positions of leadership. They receive a small stipend from the organisation to compensate them for loss of earnings on the street, and their role is to maintain communications between children and the staff. They bring children newly on the streets to the attention of staff. They are also expected to pass onto other children what they learn about such topics as hygiene and AIDS.

One of the outreach workers, supported by the organisation, takes in children – particularly girls – to her home in the suburb of Tafara. She provides informal foster care for the children, normally on a short-term basis until more permanent arrangements can be made. She arranges for their education and for talks and support from other women. This woman dedicates much of her free time to the children, and is much appreciated by them: they always speak well of her even while they are criticising other outreach workers. When asked how she manages and where she gets all the energy to look after so many homeless girls, she replied:

> *I love children. My heart aches especially when I see these young girls loitering the streets and getting exposed to all the evils of society. I want to see these young girls in school because it is their only key out of poverty, and women have for a long time been short-changed due to their uneducated status. A girl should be able to write her own letters.*

The *Girl Child Network* was launched in 1999 to represent the needs of the underprivileged girls and the broader need to redress gender imbalances evident in socio-economic, political and religious institutions. This organisation focuses on conditions in which girls are seriously hurt, such as rape, forced marriages, premarital sex and gender dimensions of AIDS. It started as a club at a school in the suburb of Chitungwiza but has grown rapidly. By the time of our research, it was operating 16 informal discussion groups with more than 1 500 members in the city.

The objectives of *Girl Child Network* are primarily to improve the self-image of girls and to empower them to resist various forms of sexual abuse. It concentrates on education and training, and includes defensive tactics like karate. It also runs a safe house that gives temporary shelter to abused girls.

Shelter Trust is a welfare organisation founded in 1987 by the Abandoned Babies sub-committee of the *Zimbabwe Council for the Welfare of Children*. It caters for young pregnant girls, including street girls, and is located in the Harare suburb of Westwood (near Kambuzuma). It gives temporary shelter to pregnant young women and prepares them for delivery; it tries to reconcile the girls with their families, and, in particular, to involve the father of the child. It also provides support for desperate women in their homes.

Mbuya Nehanda Training Institute, a former refugee camp, is situated at Melfort farm, 25 km east of Harare. It operates as a home for street children and other destitute children, giving them education and accommodation. Children are encouraged to take part in the farming projects of the Institute, which help to feed the children. The organisation has suffered from chronic financial problems, and from time to time has been short of food and other necessities for the children.

Other individuals and organisations help street children in Harare.[24] The *Presbyterian Church* provides an informal school and a feeding programme for young street children in the city centre, and study groups for older children in the Mbare suburb. The Anglican Cathedral regularly provides midday meals for destitute people, which some of the girls in our study used occasionally (children have complained of being treated without respect). The *Department of Social Welfare* tries to help where it can with limited resources and limited personnel. A variety of institutions provide homes, more or less temporary, for a very limited number of children:

---

[24] For a list of organisations and contact addresses, see *Directory of Children's Services in Zimbabwe – 2000*. Save the Children (U.K.), Harare, 2000.

early in 2002, places in such homes totalled under 100, while estimates of children sleeping on the streets were around 1 000. There are many children, like the girls in our study, who do not manage to access such help.

The study methods

Our point of entry to working with street children was Streets Ahead.[25] Rurevo worked with the organisation from December 2000 to February 2001. Through its outreach programme, she was able to contact street children, and in particular street girls, both during the day and at night, and also to assess and observe their working and living conditions. She participated in some of the activities run by the organisation, such as facilitating the access of sick street children to medical vouchers from the Department of Social Welfare. She also took part in identifying and placing some of the children in appropriate institutions. Through this participatory support rendered to the organisation, she was able to interact with street children – and street girls in particular – with minimal suspicion or mistrust on their part.

She joined Streets Ahead staff in night outreach exercises, and observed the sleeping conditions at their bases. She also observed various activities that they undertake at night, including indications of sexual activity. Although her motive was to find out about their lives, there were times when the children had problems that she could not ignore, and she helped where she could.

Outside the organisations that provide services to street children, the study was carried out in most cases within the children's own environments, with children as voluntary informants. No child was forced to take part in the study. Children who participated in the study understood its purpose. In order to protect the identity of participants, all names of children in this book are pseudonyms,

---

[25] Michael Bourdillon is a long-standing member of the Board of Directors of Streets Ahead.

Photograph courtesy of Streets Ahead

Sleeping arrangements can be as ingenious as they are basic.

and the children we write about do not appear in the photographs. Rurevo interviewed the children in a conversational and informal way, and in the language most familiar to the children, usually Shona or Ndebele. The cases presented in this book result from these interviews and observations, supported by interviews with officials from the Department of Social Welfare and the Zimbabwe Republic Police, as well as with staff in organisations helping street children.

Interviews focused on the children's backgrounds, situations and experiences. From the stories of more than twenty girls whom she met regularly, she chose for more detailed study cases that were accessible and that presented experiences that seemed representative of the lives of street girls. The girls she interviewed were chosen through contact with Streets Ahead, and because they had relatively stable bases on the streets and were available throughout the period of the study: she started interviewing some girls who had to be dropped from the study when she failed to contact them again. The children's stories that we present generally reflect what the girls told Rurevo.

The round-ups of street at the time of the study impeded our research, since some children would disappear from the streets for weeks on end. Discussions begun with certain street girls had to be abandoned when they vanished from the streets for extended periods.

The work was very distressing at times. Rurevo came across situations in which men and women were organising the prostitution of girls. A girl as young as nine was being used by her carer to obtain income through sex. Although these cases have been brought to the attention of the Department of Social Welfare and the police, the operations continue.

Although limited in scope, this study of the life experiences of street girls exposes the serious plight of these girls and the need to take their problems seriously.

🐾 The Children's Stories 🐾

Rumbidzai Rurevo

Susan and Gina

This case shows the mixed fortunes and tribulations of a 'family' that tries hard to pull together at all times against all odds. It shows that, despite living on the streets and their reliance on the fringe economy, family members might still maintain contact and support each other, socially, morally and economically. It shows, too, that young girls can be the breadwinners of a family.

Susan and Gina are sisters, aged 13 and 15 years respectively when I met them. They had been staying along the Mukuvisi River for over five years. Their home was a small shack of timber covered with plastic, about two and a half metres square, where they lived with their mother and two younger children, aged six and three. The girls come from Chipinge District, about 500 kilometres by road from Harare.

Their parents separated in 1996. Their father was never employed. Problems started when their mother thought of seeking employment on the nearby farms. She took her two girls with her to the farms, leaving their father behind. With the first wage she earned, she travelled with the girls to Harare, intending to proceed to her own parents in Shamva, 70 kilometres north-east of Harare. They arrived in Harare late in the day and could not proceed with their journey to Shamva. So they had to sleep at Mbare bus terminus with other stranded travellers and homeless people. During the night, their money and belongings were stolen. They had to beg in an attempt to raise money for their upkeep and to proceed with their journey to Shamva. One man informed the mother of the girls that a farm in Norton (40 kilometres west of Harare) was looking for people to work there as farm labourers and she took up the offer. The mother not only found employment on the farm, but also entered a relationship with this man, and sent her daughters back to their father in Chipinge.

When the girls returned home, their father was seriously ill. Their mother returned to Chipinge two months later after being deserted by the man she had been living with.

Life was not the same for Susan and Gina as their parents often fought, and their mother then decided, once more, to move out of the marital home. She took her two children back to Harare, where they could not afford rented accommodation. Consequently, they lived along Mukuvisi River, where many of Harare's homeless people live.

When Gina found employment as a baby-minder in the suburb of Epworth, they were able to rent a room in Epworth, until Gina had problems with her employer and lost her job – the employer complained of food going missing and accused her of theft, which she denied. The family had to move out of rented accommodation and returned to the Mukuvisi River.

Back at Mukuvisi with no stable source of income, the girls and their mother lived from hand to mouth. They sold anything that they could lay their hands on, from rags to plastic packets and vegetables. They were also exposed to gambling with cards.

Although they did not call it prostitution, the girls were not comfortable talking about their sexual behaviour. They were not open on the topic, especially Gina, the elder sister, who seemed to bear all the responsibility for the welfare of the family. They only disclosed that at times their mother told them to be 'nice to men so that they would not starve'. Gina especially felt let down by her mother, who not only kept having children by different fathers but also incurred debts in the purchase of *kachasu* (illegally distilled liquor).

Owing to the high mobility in the life experiences of the two girls, they had been in and out of school. On the streets of Harare, they met some friends who told them about Streets Ahead. They sought help from the organisation and were enrolled at the Presbyterian Church in Mbare, where they joined a study group. Because of their living conditions in the squatter settlement, their school attendance was irregular, exacerbated by the fact that their mother did not view education as priority in comparison to the challenges of survival.

Streets Ahead felt that, if meaningful change was to be achieved in the children's lives, they had to be removed from their living environment. Temporary shelter was found for them with a foster parent while more permanent arrangements were being sought. Their foster parent's home is constantly referred as *'kumba kwemastreet kids'* [the home of street kids], and the term 'street kids' is considered derogatory and not liked by the children. The girls do not seem to mind, however, this categorisation of their home.

After placement at the Streets Ahead foster home, the girls were enrolled at Mbuya Nehanda Training Institute, where they boarded during the school term and returned to the city under the care of the foster parent during school holidays. As the girls were used to their freedom and independence on the streets, they failed to adjust quickly to the restrictive rules and regulations of the Institute. Moreover, food shortages and lack of personal care by understaffed caregivers encouraged the girls, together with other children, to desert the Institute. The girls went back into the foster home and vowed never to leave for any other place. They have now been living with their foster mother for more than two years.

At first they attended informal night school, since they had no birth certificates, which are required for enrolment in a regular school. By the time of our study, and with the help of Streets Ahead, they had obtained the necessary certificates and were attending full time day school. Both were in grade seven, the last grade in primary school. Initially they found it difficult to cope with the workload and to fit into the system, and at times they were absent from classes. Constant counselling from volunteers seems to have helped. Reports of absenteeism became less frequent, and they now show interest in, and commitment to, their schoolwork by doing their homework with minimal supervision. While Gina sees education as stepping-stone to a better future, her younger sister thinks otherwise. Susan feels that the organisations that help street children should do everything for them because they owe their existence to the presence of children in the streets.

Not only did the girls adjust towards life in a family home, but they also kept close contact with their biological family at Mukuvisi, visiting regularly there at weekends. They enjoyed family bonds as well as the street freedom when they visited their family at Mukuvisi, without compromising the gains achieved in the home, where they were able to enjoy a more normal childhood.

At the end of the study period, the girls appeared happy and contented, and it appeared that the intervention had been helpful and successful. Subsequent to the study, however, Susan left the foster home to be with a boyfriend. Gina started coming back late from her visits home at the weekends, and finally failed to return. Both are now back on the streets.

Pamela and Patience

Like Gina and Susan, the problems of Pamela and Patience originate with a broken home. In this case, they are openly utilised by their primary caregiver for income.

The two girls are cousins, aged nine and eleven when I met them, and were living under the care of their maternal grandmother in the city.

Pamela's mother lived in the Mabvuku suburb of Harare with a man other than the girl's father, and Pamela's father lived in Gweru, 275 kilometres from Harare, with another woman. When Pamela was conceived, her mother was working as a housemaid for the man who impregnated her. Subsequently, the mother was sent away by Pamela's father, who never took care of the child.

Pamela grew up in the suburb of Silobela in Bulawayo under the care of her grandmother, Mbuya MaMoyo, who was living with a man who was not formally her husband. After this man chased her away from his home, MaMoyo came to Harare with her grandchild. Her relatives were not willing to take her in because of her reputation of moving in and out to live with different men. Initially, she rented a shack in the Harare suburb of Epworth, but moved into the city centre when her shack and belongings were destroyed by rain.

Pamela's mother married. The husband (Pamela's stepfather) did not mind if Pamela visited for a few days, but he never welcomed her into the home since, given her mobile background with her grandmother, he believed she would be a bad influence on his children. So Pamela remained with her grandmother.

Mbuya MaMoyo used to collect waste paper for resale directly. She also sold marijuana, and other illicit brews to supplement her income. Initially, when she lived in Epworth, she would commute regularly from there to town. After her shack had been destroyed, she moved into the city centre permanently, where she survives mainly by begging. Now she organises street children to collect waste paper and plastic for her, which she passes on to those who sell directly to recycling companies.

Patience is Pamela's cousin (their mothers are sisters), and Patience's mother has not been successful in marriage. Patience used to live with her paternal aunt. When the aunt died, Patience, now in fifth grade, dropped out of school and had to join her mother who, at the time, was staying with her boyfriend (or 'husband') in Epworth. After the move to her mother's, Patience no longer attended school, although the mother kept giving excuses about plans for Patience to continue her education. The 'stepfather' appeared unwilling to pay for the girl's schooling.

The couple had been having problems, which increased when Patience moved in with them. They were constantly fighting and the 'husband' would often remind Patience that she was not his child and so should be grateful for the food and roof over her head. He would also often sarcastically refer to Mbuya MaMoyo's lifestyle (implying that Patience's mother was lucky to have a man who had not only made her a wife but also given her a decent home, unlike her mother who had moved from place to place and man to man). Patience ran away to join her grandmother[26] and Pamela in the streets because she felt she was the major cause of the fights between her mother and the 'husband' and because she wanted to save her mother's relationship.

She did not like living in the streets because it is very cold at night and she missed decent meals with a family and proper sleep that other children have. She did not like the long hours she had to spend carrying her younger brother on her back as

---

[26] I have told the story as related by the girls. A social worker questioned whether any of the girls used by 'grandmother' were in fact related to her.

a ploy for sympathy when begging. (When passers-by saw her with a hungry looking infant, they were drawn to give more.)

At night, at the insistence of her grandmother, she had to entertain street boys. She did not want to say how she entertained them. Some street boys informed us, however, that they surrender to Mbuya MaMoyo some of the money they beg or earn through minding cars. In return, they are given food and the right to have sex with the two cousins and other street girls in her care. I was warned that Mbuya MaMoyo does not entertain strangers or answer questions. She has unequivocally told Patience and Pamela that they must not refuse to entertain those boys who surrender part of their earnings to her unless they want to starve. Sometimes the girls had to entertain old men who give large sums of money to their grandmother. The young girls had heard about AIDS and that it kills, but they did not seem to know much about it and had not bothered to find out, largely because of the pressure to eke out an existence.[27]

Whilst Pamela has never had a stable family life and did not want to talk much about her mother, Patience was more ready to talk and felt she was responsible for her mother's marital problems. In June 2000, however, subsequent to the research, Patience's mother joined the girls and their grandmother on the streets: she was ill and had a young baby.

---

[27] *Daily News* (6 January, 2002, 'Streets turned into brothels') reported a woman, herself on the streets, who welcomed and protected young girls when they first arrived on the streets and then used them in her sex business with male motorists and with street boys. The report stated that her operation comprised seven girls, one as young as twelve. Two rescued girls claimed that they had reported their situation to police, but that no action had been taken: they were told it was their own fault for being on the streets. The report mentioned an incident in which two of the girls found their way to a home for street children, and she took them back by persuading the person in charge that she was a relative and had school places for them. The woman disappeared from the streets for a while after this publicity, only to continue her enterprise later.

As in the first case of Gina and Susan, Pamela and Patience dropped out of school owing to lack of finance and work the streets instead to contribute to the family livelihood. They occasionally visited Streets Ahead but, at the time of the research, they were not part of any regular programme. In both cases, the families were desperately poor. In neither case could the children depend on the adult world for sustenance or for moral support.

Babra

The case of Babra illustrates how extended family networks can be destroyed by economic factors. The family's resources were depleted by the illness of Babra's father, and his relatives deprived her mother of what remained, driving her onto the streets in poverty.

. Babra is the youngest girl in a family of six children, and was fifteen at the time of the study. She had four older sisters, aged between seventeen and 26, who were all married. Her younger brother lived in town with her and their homeless mother. One of Babra's sisters, Mercy, aged about twenty, was married to a street boy and alternated between living on the streets and staying in a rented room in the poor suburb of Hatcliffe. Mercy had three children of her own.

Babra was born in Chinhoyi and grew up in the care of her maternal grandmother. Her paternal rural home is Mount Darwin although she does not know most of her father's relatives. Her father died in 1996 after a long struggle with tuberculosis, having exhausted most of the family resources in search of a cure. His relatives threw her mother out of her matrimonial home, accusing her of bewitching him. Babra's mother's refusal to accept overtures from one of her husband's brothers, who wished to inherit her as a wife, incensed the paternal relatives. There were also tensions resulting from the failure of the father's relatives to pay marriage payments in full. This hostility drove Babra's mother to take her children to her own relatives in Chinhoyi where she thought she would be welcome. Babra was very young when she left Mount Darwin with her mother.

Babra left school when her mother had an argument with her brother (Babra's uncle) and was told to go away with all her children. Because the mother had nowhere to live within Chinhoyi, and perceiving job opportunities to be limited there, she left for Harare. In Harare, she could not find employment and was forced to live on the streets with her children, some of whom have married and settled with their husbands in regular housing, but some of whom have married street boys[28] and so stay with her on the streets with their children. The family sleeps with other street people on pavements near the railway station.

At the time of this study, Babra's sister, Mercy, was attending sewing lessons in Mbare sponsored by Streets Ahead so that she could be self-sustaining economically, and able to raise her children. She had problems with the theory of cutting and designing, but was doing well in the practical sewing. When she was living in town rather than at Hatcliffe, Mercy used to leave her children with Babra and their mother whilst attending sewing lessons. Mercy's children would, in turn, be used as bait to beg for money.

Mercy's husband spent most of his time on the streets guarding and cleaning cars and making money for his family in any way he could. Mercy occasionally joined her husband on the streets, and thus spent some time with her young sister Babra and their mother, begging in the city centre. While there, apart from begging, Mercy surreptitiously engaged in prostitution to supplement her husband's income.

---

[28] Although street people do not go through the formalities of marriage, they often establish relatively stable relations, which involves adopting the terms 'husband' and 'wife', and conveys obligations of support. Men usually claim exclusive sexual rights in their 'wives'. See the comment of Shamiso below.

Before being introduced to Babra, I used to see her with her mother and nieces, sitting by Africa Unity Square and sending children to beg for money. Babra was a shy but jovial young girl who hardly spoke unless spoken to. I used to wonder how she managed to say, '*Sister ndokumbirawo pondo nditenge chingwa.*' [Sister, I am asking for help[29] to buy bread]. This is a common request from street children, advanced to anyone who passes through Africa Unity Square.

As I talked to her more often and observed her interactions from afar, I discovered that, despite being reserved, Babra seemed well adjusted and accepted her surroundings. She had a steady boyfriend or 'husband', and at the beginning of study she was about eight months pregnant – by the end she had a child. Her husband was a homeless street boy, who watched over cars and used what little money he earned to look after Babra and her mother.

Babra's love life, however, was not without problems. On about three occasions when I visited her, she had a swollen face or a blue eye. At first, I thought it was due to her pregnancy but soon learnt that it was because she had been fighting with her 'husband'. Her younger brother once said to me, '*Akarohwa nemurume wake... mukandipa pondo ndinokuudzai zvakaitika.*' [She was beaten by her husband, and if you give me two dollars I will tell you what happened.] In some instances, it was reported that Babra's husband beat her in front of his mother-in-law.

Often, Babra was chastised by her mother for what initially appeared to be talking too much in public, although with time I learnt that the fights between the two of them were often about Babra's infidelity. She would have sexual relations with other men or street children to supplement her income, saying that her husband did not always bring home all his earnings

---

as he spends some on glue for sniffing, kachasu, and marijuana. A woman (especially in her condition) needs an income of her own, she added, to prepare for emergencies, and, furthermore, she accused her husband of being unfaithful too. Babra's mother knew about her daughter's relations with men other than her husband, and did not prevent these relationships, which explains why Babra's husband often acted disrespectfully towards his mother-in-law, something that is not acceptable in the Shona culture.

Babra acknowledged that life on the street is not easy, since the means of survival for girls like her are often judged by the public as morally repugnant in comparison to those of their boy counterparts. A good woman cannot live on the streets. Any woman who lives on the streets is considered by society to be sexually available and therefore cheap. This is further supported by the fact that girls, unlike boys, are not allowed to guard or wash cars or tout for passengers for emergency taxis, for these are regarded strictly as male domains. She said:

Sisi upenyu hwemumugwagwa hwakaoma, tinongobatabatawo kuti tirarame, asi zvinorema. [My sister, life is in the streets is tough, one has to devise several strategies to survive, but it is heavy.]

Besides limited survival strategies for street girls, Babra pointed out that street girls live in constant fear of being rounded up by police for institutionalisation. Police also arrest them for loitering, and municipal officials confiscate their wares and belongings as a way of clearing the city of destitutes and illegal vendors.

Thus, for Babra, girls have to rely on men who are either boyfriends or clients for food, clothes and other necessities of life. She said that even with a steady boyfriend or husband, a street girl at times resorts to prostitution in order to supplement the meagre income the two as a couple might be earning.

Babra also tried to earn an honest living. Occasionally, I observed her selling boiled eggs and popcorn or cigarettes to other street children. She boiled the eggs at Streets Ahead. This was to help her raise money to prepare for her unborn baby. Sometimes people felt pity for her due to her pregnant state and gave her money or left-over food.

Babra did not want to spend the rest of her life in the streets. She wanted to enrol with the Streets Ahead programme that sponsors girls to attend sewing classes. She hoped that she would find employment as a tailor or buy her own sewing machine and become self-employed.

By the end of the research, Babra's mother claimed that she had made peace with her brother and that she could return to her mother's (Babra's grandmother's) house in Chinhoyi. The pressure to speak of a secure home followed an incident over Babra's child, who had been taken in by the Department of Social Welfare after the child was used by another sick and destitute women as 'bait' for begging.[30] I was involved in the negotiations with the officers on her behalf and her child's right to be with its natural mother instead of in a children's home. Babra was counselled and advised to leave the streets and take accommodation offered by her seventeen-year-old sister in Epworth. While promising to take up the offer for the welfare of her child, Babra was still in the streets despite warnings that her child would be taken away if she was seen in the streets. The child has since died.

---

[30] This action followed a story in a press about an infant who was left behind when an ambulance team took the mother, a street-girl, for emergency hospital treatment. The child was being cared for by other women on the streets, but had been three days without being bathed. Reporters commented that the 'street mothers' could not explain why they had not returned the child to its mother as soon as they had located her. See *The Herald*, 31 January, 2001, 'Ambulance leaves baby on streets'; and 1 February, 2001, 'Baby left in streets is cared for by destitute women'.

Buhle

The case of Buhle illustrates how fostering can result in girls being exploited as domestic servants. It also shows how lack of communication between children and adults can sour relationships. Again, prostitution is one of the strategies for survival.

Buhle was seventeen at the time this study, and had been in the streets for about five months after running away from the aunt she had lived with in Harare. Buhle and her friends established their base at the main station of the National Railways of Zimbabwe. One of her friends had a child and was herself sickly. Buhle and her friends used public facilities such as toilets at the National Railways of Zimbabwe, to bath and wash their clothes. Buhle's group of friends, both girls and boys, was predominantly made up of young people from the same region, namely Bulawayo and Gweru.

Buhle was born in Mbembesi, about 40 km from Bulawayo, and was the fourth child in a family of eight. Both her parents live in Bulawayo. Her father was a general hand at a factory, while her mother was a cleaner at Mpilo General Hospital. Buhle was not bright at school, and she developed a hatred for it that led to her absconding from classes before dropping out altogether when she was in Form 3. She liked dancing and drama and had been teased by her classmates and teachers about taking more interest in dancing than in academic subjects.[31] Buhle blamed the education system for not nurturing students with non-academic talents. After she had dropped out of formal school, her parents enrolled her at night school so that she could continue with her education. This was cheaper for them because she could do domestic chores when everyone was away from home, and she was free to do as she pleased during the day. She had two brothers at

---

[31] Poor performance is frequently punished in Zimbabwean schools. Such punishment is often arbitrary and very humiliating for the children.

secondary school and two others at primary school. Her two elder sisters were married: one lived in Botswana with her husband while the other was involved in cross-border trading. Buhle's elder brother was an illegal immigrant in South Africa and rarely comes home.

When she dropped out of school, Buhle wanted to go to South Africa, in particular to live in Gauteng in Johannesburg, popularly known as 'Egoli' (the City of Gold). So the night school suited her plans well as she could do piece jobs during the day and raise money for the bus fare across the border. She used to work as a stand-in at the flea market stall of her mother's friend in Bulawayo when the latter had gone shopping in South Africa. This was Buhle's introduction into the informal economy.

Buhle's plans to raise money for travel were jeopardised when her father's recently widowed, childless sister asked her to come to Harare to help out with domestic chores. Buhle came on the understanding that she would continue with night school, and help her aunt in exchange for a wage. Although she was enrolled for night school, she never attended regularly as her aunt kept her too busy. When she asked her aunt about school or the money owed to her, the aunt replied that she was doing her niece a favour by letting her go to school at all, as the food and shelter she received was more than adequate payment for the work she did.

Eventually Buhle decided that she would be better off on the streets, where she would be free of the demands of her aunt, and where she could earn an independent income.

I tried to verify the story with the aunt, who lived in the suburb of Kuwadzana and was self-employed in cross-border trading. The aunt alleged that she had asked for her niece to live with her so that Buhle could house-sit for her, run her flea market stall while she was away, and also take care of the general household chores. It had also been agreed with Buhle's parents that the aunt would remit some money to the parents to assist with the upkeep of Buhle's siblings. She had not yet sent any money, however, because she had been ill for some time. As to the whereabouts of Buhle, the aunt alleged that she had disappeared after a misunderstanding over the issue of boyfriends. The aunt also said that Buhle was a troublesome child, who needed close and strict monitoring, which her parents had failed to provide. She was not very surprised to hear that Buhle was living on the streets, as the girl had given her nothing but headaches since arriving in Harare. She indicated that she thought that Buhle had gone back to her parents in Bulawayo, although she would not say what had given her this impression. The aunt felt that Buhle was spoiled; Buhle thought she was being short-changed by the adult world.

As to how she was surviving on the streets, Buhle summarised her survival strategies in one sentence:

> *Sisi njengoba ngiyinkazana engelamsebenzi oqondileyo ucabanga ukuthi ngiphila njani?* [Sister, since I am a girl living on the streets with no other means of generating income, how do you think I earn that income or my living?]

There is no doubt that Buhle survived on prostitution, although she refused to elaborate. Buhle and other girls living on the streets lack the capacity to earn money with which to buy food and other necessities of life, so they often find it convenient to have boyfriends and other male clients to provide for them.

While the girls willingly share sexual favours with some of the boys and men, other groups of boys and men abuse them sexually. Buhle claimed that the police do not spare them: they are arrested for loitering if found walking the streets at night and, sometimes, instead charging them, the police extort sexual favours from the girls in return for freedom, especially when they do not have money to pay the fine. Buhle had been arrested for loitering three times during the five months that she had been on the streets. On the first occasion, one of the girls in their group paid her fine because she had no money on her. For the two other arrests, she had learned where to keep extra cash in her underwear in case she got into trouble.

Buhle complained of the physical exploitation that she and other girls living on the streets had to endure from street boys, who beat them if they refused their sexual advances. One group of street boys gave protection to Buhle and her friends, while a rival gang gave them problems.

When things were extremely hard and Buhle could not earn enough money, she joined other destitute people at the Anglican Cathedral for the lunch and tea offered freely there by volunteers.

On the subject of her ambitions, Buhle said she had tried to go to school but now felt too old to go back and start where she had left off. Consequently, she felt that her family would not accept her back, or if they did, that they would always refer negatively to this episode in her life. She valued her family and wanted to maintain contact, but thought it would be better if she went to South Africa for a while, and returned when everyone had forgotten about this episode, and once she had achieved some success in her life. Buhle repeated that she was not a troublemaker, as people might want to think. She had no interest in school, but felt that she could earn an honest living through acting and dancing.

Some of her friends used to go to Streets Ahead but then stopped. Asked about the organisation, Buhle said she had heard about it and the kind of help it offers. She indicated she had not bothered to seek help from the organisation because her mission was to go to South Africa and not be reunited with her family, as they might try to encourage her to do, or immediately go back to school. During the early days, when all she had wanted was to go back to Bulawayo, she had sought help from the Department of Social Welfare, but she did not like the way they spoke to her and had vowed never to go back

When my fieldwork ended, Buhle was still living on the streets but was on speaking terms with her aunt. She had made no effort to seek help from any of the service providers. She said she was planning to go home.[32] Buhle seemed, however, well adapted to street life. She avoided organisations that could help her because she was comfortable with her lifestyle.

In Buhle's case, it was not so much a broken family that drove the girl onto the streets, as the social expectation that girls could be pledged to do service for a relative. This kind of worker is not a formal employee and does not enjoy the legal rights of an employee to fixed hours, time off and regular wages. Buhle felt she was being exploited, and this is often the case in such situations. There were clearly problems in the relationships between Buhle and the adults in her life. There was also a problem with her schooling. A rigid emphasis on academic learning allows little flexibility for children with other capabilities and interests, which appeared to concern neither her school nor her parents, both of whom had poor jobs and thought of academic schooling as a way to a white-collar position for their daughter and a brighter future.

Buhle was openly involved in prostitution, and was aware of the social stigma this involves, which made it difficult for her to return to her family. The public looked down on her group of friends. On one occasion, when I was looking for her at the railway station, an official there asked why I bothered with such hopeless and good-for-nothing people. He said that all they were capable of was using their bodies to earn an income instead of doing something more honest with their lives.

---

[32] Since I was associated with Streets Ahead's outreach programme, it is likely that her motive for telling me she was going home was to distract attention from Streets Ahead's outreach and peer staff, who might otherwise come and encourage her to get involved in their activities.

Buhle's case is not an isolated one. Some children live on the streets because of peer pressure or love of adventure, and others are there because they have been frustrated by an education system that is not flexible enough to accommodate different talents.

Shylet

This case of Shylet illustrates the weakening of the extended family network and values because of economic hardships and nuclearisation of families. The mother never revealed the identity of the father of the child. Consequently, the child failed to get assistance from the father and his kin, who might have been willing to assist in times of need.

Shylet's mother never married and her family never knew the identity of Shylet's father. It is not clear whether the mother knew who the father was. When she became pregnant with Shylet, she was working as a barmaid at a service centre in Gutu, a town about 250 kilometres south of Harare. Her employer did not want to pay her whilst she was on maternity leave, so she lost her job. After Shylet was born, her mother had to leave her new-born baby in the care of its reluctant grandmother, as she had to look elsewhere for ways to earn a living. The mother had no educational qualifications and became involved in prostitution to be able to look after her child.

According to Shylet, it was only when her mother began to remit money home that the grandmother showed affection towards her granddaughter. This was short-lived, however, as Shylet's mother became sick and died of AIDS when Shylet was barely six years old. Living with her grandmother became a living nightmare as she was constantly referred to as '*mwana wehure*' [child of a prostitute]. When she was about seven, her aunt in Harare took her into her household, but treated her no better than her grandmother had done. Shylet was attending school irregularly, as her maternal relatives did not see her schooling as a priority, mainly as she was not their child. Because she was often absent from school, she was always behind in her schoolwork, so she began to resent school. Her classmates too often teased her for always paying her fees late and having an incomplete uniform. Although her teacher intervened and punished the culprits, Shylet felt she had been rejected by the system and perceived herself as a misfit. She became rebellious and violent towards other children. She would miss more lessons and finally dropped out of school when she was in Grade 4.

Once she left school, her aunt made her do all the household chores and sell sweets and cigarettes at the Mbare market. The aunt said that her niece had to earn her keep and welfare: this was city life, which is expensive, and everyone has to make a financial contribution. Her aunt beat Shylet if she brought home insufficient money. Shylet learnt to gamble to increase the earnings she took home. She ran away from her aunt's house when she could not take the beatings any more and teamed up with her friends who lived by the Mukuvisi River.

To survive, she used to gamble, sell *kachasu* and sleep with men. She contracted a sexually transmitted infection and had to seek medical attention at a clinic in Mbare. Staff at the clinic where she was treated referred her to Streets Ahead's outreach programme to get her off the streets.

The outreach programme at Streets Ahead reunited her with her aunt. The organisation undertook to pay her school fees and other school-related expenses, on condition that she lived with her aunt and that the latter did not abuse her. At first, Shylet enrolled in a study group in Mbare run by the Presbyterian Church, where she attended class regularly. With time, her aunt became resentful about her lack of contribution to the household, and sometimes Shylet would be denied food and told to eat books, especially when food was scarce. On the other hand, if there was more food, she would be told to eat all the food even if she had eaten more than enough. These living conditions made her frustrated and she started missing classes again. She began gambling and vending, and dropped out of school.

Shylet never told Streets Ahead that she had dropped out of school. Rather, she would tell them that she was attending class in the morning or afternoon depending on what time they found her in the streets. When they finally discovered that she was no longer in school, the outreach programme requested permission from the aunt to place Shylet in a children's home. She was taken to Mbuya Nehanda, where she stayed for two terms before she ran away with other children. She cited lack of food, beatings by members of staff, and peer pressure as some of the reasons why she ran away.

When I met Shylet, she was attending school while staying in the foster home of the Streets Ahead worker. She did not like school because she would get low grades and was nicknamed '*mustreet-kid*' by her classmates. She had repeated a class or grade each time she resumed school, so at the age of thirteen she was in Grade 5 with eleven-year-olds. She also had problems acquiring a birth certificate, as her aunt wanted nothing more to do with her. Months after the research, Shylet had dropped out of school again and had gone back to the streets.

Tambu

One of the points illustrated by the case of Shylet is the problems children face when they are born of loose sexual relationships outside marriage. Such problems were even more severe in the case of Tambu, who was also conceived out of wedlock, and suffered when her mother died while she was young. The ideals of our society require mating to take place within a stable, religiously and traditionally sanctioned marriage. In practice, extra-marital relationships are widespread, and poor people rarely trouble themselves with formal marriage commitments. The relationship of Tambu's parents was never religiously or traditionally sanctioned, and consequently, her relatives wanted nothing to do with the child upon her mother's death. Because responsibility is constantly shifting among relatives and the surviving parent, children are sometimes not provided for, resulting in irregular school attendance, and having to fend for themselves at a tender age. This case shows how the surviving parent's inability to deal with the responsibilities of single parenthood can jeopardise children's future.

Tambu was about six years old. Her mother was dead, and her father's whereabouts were not known, although his identity was known. He was said to be an alcoholic. Tambu had been under the care of her father's brother and his wife. Often while Tambu's uncle was away at work, her aunt would physically and emotionally abuse her, and even deny her food. Policemen picked her up after she had wandered beyond familiar grounds in search of food in the streets and got lost. They took her to the house of the outreach worker of Streets Ahead.

A drama group at Streets Ahead: the search for food.

When I first met Tambu, she had been at this foster house for about a week. She looked physically malnourished. She hardly spoke and seemed to be suspicious of everyone, except the foster mother. Tambu told her foster mother once, after seeing some romantic scenes on television, what had been done to her by one of her uncles (her aunt's brother) and one of her cousins.

> *Kuita sezviya zvataiita nasekuru… nabhudhi… asi vakati ndisaudza munhu. Vakati ndikaudza munhu ndinofa.* [It is like what we used to do with my uncle and cousin brother and they said I should not tell anyone or else I will die.]

It was clear that Tambu had been sexually abused by some of the people she should have been able to trust.

As there were already too many people at the foster home, accommodation had to be sought for Tambu elsewhere. A place was found at the Girl Child Network in Chitungwiza, most suitable in this case as their main purpose is to help girls who have been sexually abused. I accompanied the outreach workers who took Tambu to the Girl Child Network.

At the Girl Child Network, Tambu was given temporary shelter while they investigated her background. Contact was made with her uncle who acknowledged that his wife had not welcomed Tambu since that meant another mouth to feed. He wanted the Girl Child Network to accommodate Tambu until more permanent arrangements could be made. He professed ignorance about the alleged sexual abuse.

Meanwhile during my regular visits to the Girl Child Network, I established that Tambu was enrolled at the nearest pre-school and was getting well adapted to her environment. She always asked me when I would take her back home to the foster parent in Tafara.

This case further illustrates the pressures in the city on an extended family network, which is no guarantee for assistance in times of need. If the extended family assists, it views such assistance only as a stopgap measure, since members of the extended family now tend to be viewed as a burden. The case also illustrates the difficulty of trying to accommodate desperate children in over-stretched welfare facilities.

Shamiso

The case of Shamiso demonstrates how lack of accommodation in high-density suburbs and squatter camps can send children onto the streets. Overcrowding can force children to grow up accustomed to the street environment at an early age, and can lead to teenage pregnancy for girls.

Shamiso was seventeen years old and had an eight-month-old son. She lived on the streets. Her parents lived in one of the rough wooden houses in Dzivarasekwa Extension. She had run away from home to live with her boyfriend, Max, who at that time was living in Epworth, where he was renting a room with some friends. Max had moved out of his parent's home in Dzivarasekwa Extension because he felt he was too old to continue sharing a room with his sisters and young brothers. Shamiso tried to go back home when she was pregnant, but for this reason was driven away by her parents. In the Shona culture if a girl elopes with her boyfriend, she is not allowed back until the boyfriend comes to inform the girl's parents formally that he has their daughter, paving the way for negotiations about marriage payments. Since Max had not done this, Shamiso's parents sent her back to him.

On the other hand, Max's parents did not welcome her into their house as they felt that the couple was too young to marry. Shamiso was left with no option except to join her boyfriend. Sharing a room with Max's friends became problematic, however, so the couple moved to the streets in the city centre near the railway station, where they have been living since 1999 as husband and wife.

During her pregnancy, Streets Ahead facilitated free medical care and treatment for Shamiso from the Department of Social Welfare. The organisation also linked her with Shelter Trust, where she went to deliver her baby.

Shamiso was elected as a street peer by other street children and outreach staff of Streets Ahead, and, as a result, has been helping new arrivals on the streets, especially young girls, protecting them from abuse by street boys and homeless men. She identified new arrivals, whom she looked after during the night with the help of other street peers.

Of the street girls I met and talked to, Shamiso was the most experienced in street life. She knew how to manipulate her way around the street community to meet her needs. The organisations Streets Ahead and Shelter Trust have worked hard in trying to reconcile her with her family. The two organisations successfully persuaded her parents to take their daughter back home, even though there was no marriage payment from their 'son-in-law'. Shamiso had given Shelter Trust the impression that she was now living at home with her parents. In fact, she was living with her husband, who sometimes found temporary jobs: she therefore lived on the street, but left the street temporarily when they could afford to pay rent for a room.

Shamiso survived on the small allowance she was given by Streets Ahead for her role as a street peer educator, as well as from selling cigarettes to other street children and the income from her husband. Asked how other girls survive on the streets, she said that prostitution was very common among street girls. Most girls depend on men. Generally, a street girl is paired up with a street boy or homeless man for protection and security. The man assumes responsibility for her welfare and up-keep. Some girls supplement their incomes and those of their spouses through begging and small-scale vending.

Although Shamiso seemed well adapted to street life, she did not wish to spend the rest of her life there. She wanted to go back to school or to get a job, even as a domestic worker, so that she can look after her child and give him a decent upbringing, not in the streets but at home and attending school like other children of his age. Realistically, she pointed out, however, that it was difficult for a street girl to find employment, especially as a domestic worker: the moment a potential employer hears that a girl has been on the streets, they assume that she is lazy and liable to steal. Her long-term plans were to run her own business if she could find a sponsor. She wanted to do informal catering whereby she would prepare food at home and sell by arrangement either to organisations or to omnibus drivers and their touts at bus termini. Shamiso perceived herself as mature and responsible when I met her. She had made a mistake and fallen pregnant because of peer pressure, but she had reformed as evidenced by the responsibility that Streets Ahead entrusted to her.[33]

She pointed out that intervention programmes offered by some institutions to girls were of little use to them. She wished that these organisations would identify one's talent and then groom that girl along her interests. Shamiso blamed lack of consultation between organisations and children. She claimed that most children take part in these programmes because there is no other option, and out of fear that organisations will think that they do not want to improve their plight. She argued that she had given Shelter Trust the impression that she was back at home because she wanted to enrol in their skills training centre, 'mufandichimuka'.

It remained to be seen when she would enrol for the programme: she had showed no urgency in the matter before the research ended.

---

[33] Two years later, she had a child and was pregnant again.

Cynthia and Catherine

My last two cases are children who have supportive homes to go to at night, but spend much of their time working on the streets.

When I first met Cynthia and Catherine, Cynthia was aged sixteen and completing Form 3 at Kambuzuma High School. Catherine was eleven and had stopped going to school when she was in Grade 7 of primary school.

After several visits to Catherine, I began to understand the reasons for her working on the streets. Their father was retrenched when the company for which he had worked for several years was forced into liquidation. With his retrenchment package, he established a butchery at a rural growth point, to sustain the livelihood of his family. The project realised good returns, earning him more money than he had earned as a worker, but soon he began to neglect his family, spending most of the money on women. He became abusive towards his family and regularly beat his wife. He was not interested in educating the girls as he felt this would not bring him any returns, since the girls would be married and therefore benefit other families.

In one beating, his wife lost two teeth, and the family decided to leave. She was advised by her husband's relatives to stay with her own relatives for some time in the Harare suburb of Rugare. The children's mother had to take her two daughters with her because their father did not want to keep the girls: according to him, girls were good for nothing except prostitution or bringing home children born out of wedlock.

The mother's relatives could only look after her and her children for a short period because of the economic hardships of high inflation, the escalation of food prices, and the shortage of accommodation. The family now rents two rooms in Rugare and operates a fruit and vegetable stall in town by the bus terminus near the Central Police Charge Office.

Soon after the family settled in Rugare, the children's mother became seriously ill and was bedridden for more than six months. It was because of this illness that Catherine opted to drop out of school to enable her sister to continue with schooling until she had written her O-level examinations in Form 4. Catherine decided to continue operating her mother's fruit and vegetable stall in town. Since the mother could no longer fend for the family, Catherine took full responsibility for the family welfare. The girls have become determined to educate each other, with encouragement from their mother.

Catherine's day started early. Every third day, she had to be at Mbare Musika market by six o'clock to buy vegetables and fruit for sale: she had to be there early to buy the best goods at reasonable prices. She did not go daily because she alternated with her mates: they bought on behalf of each other. She also had to set up her stall early in the morning as she targeted customers during the early morning peak hours when business was brisk, especially for fruit. After the early morning rush hour, about mid-morning, she caught up with sleep before lunchtime, when her stall became busy again.

Sometimes, on her way home in the evening, she took a ride on the evening train to Bulawayo, especially if she did not have enough money for the bus fare. She had to be in the company of another person, either her sister or an elderly woman, since she dropped off far away from their home and it was not safe for her to walk the remaining distance alone.

Catherine's life in the streets was not easy for a girl of her age. Her major complaint was about the weight of her wares, which she had to carry on her head from the market to the commuter omnibuses that take her to town. She constantly had to dodge the police when they rounded up fruit and vegetable vendors on the pretext of public health. At the same time, she had to give a good explanation as to why she was not at school, to the police or anyone who wished to know. Because she operated from a designated municipal area, harassment by municipal police was minimal compared to that experienced by vendors who operate outside of these points.

Her mother's friends kept an eye on her and were always on the lookout for anyone who might want to take advantage of her. Catherine was grateful for their support and commented:

These women are like mother hens to me. I am grateful for their support. If it were not for them, my mother would have died and my sister would have been out of school. They contributed a great deal towards my mother's medication. Sometimes I wander and play in town, only to come back to find that they will have sold some of my wares on my behalf in my absence.

On how she felt about dropping out of school while her sister continued with her education, Catherine said she did not mind taking responsibility even though she was the younger one.

My sister is about to finish school, and if she gets a better job she will be able to send me to school and look after our mother. I have to look after her now and I await the same from her. Moreover, I want to prove my father wrong. I want to prove that girls are as good and responsible as boys are. I want to be a lawyer when I grow up. I want my father to pay for what he did to us, especially to my mother. I know that one day he will come crawling to us begging for help.

By the end of the study, the children's mother was able to move about and undertake light menial work at home. She could sell small items like frozen drinks popularly known as freezits, and other items such as popcorn, sweets, and vegetables from her very small garden.

Cynthia does all the household chores before and after school. She helps her sister in town, especially during weekends and at month-end, when demand for fruit and vegetables is high. Sundays are devoted to worship and to family interaction.

I interviewed Cynthia less frequently, since she spent less time on the streets. I learnt from her that she had to work hard to ensure that she always excels in whatever she does. A well-wisher from her church paid exam fees for her O-levels and she was working very hard so that she would not let her benefactor down.

Cynthia woke up early in the morning, cleaned the house, and prepared breakfast for herself and her mother before she went to school. She did not participate in any extra-mural activities at school (unless they were compulsory) because of her obligations at home, looking after her mother, and generally being in charge of the household. Cynthia also had to do all her homework, either at school early in the morning or at home in the evenings by the light of a candle or paraffin lamp, because their lodgings were not electrified. At the time of the study, paraffin was in short supply, and thus more often than not Cynthia had to get to school early in the morning to do her homework. Sometimes she did her homework at a friend's house, especially when preparing for examinations. Cynthia felt that she was lucky to have such a supportive and close-knit small family, of her sister and mother. She had this to say:

> When our mother became seriously sick, I had to attend school irregularly in order to take care of her. I could not let Catherine do it because she is the breadwinner. It was only when our mother's sister came to stay with us for a short while that things got better... I wish to be an accountant and earn lots of money so that I can look after my sister and mother...

These children had a good family home, and the sisters and their mother were supportive of each other. They did not live on the streets, but the younger girl nevertheless spent most of her life on the streets. While she was deprived of schooling for the time being, she and her family seemed genuinely to benefit from her work – unlike many of the other cases.

Kumbirai and Carol

Carol is the subject of our final case. In order to understand her situation, we need to include her elder brother, Kumbirai. Like Catherine, Kumbirai and Carol illustrate the lifestyles of children of the streets who come from a poor and hardworking background. They had a home, but regularly worked on the streets. Although the children did not enjoy a leisured childhood like children from well-off families, they were happy and contented. They did not seem to mind that, while other children were playing, they had to work to contribute to the upkeep of their family and their own education.

The parents of the two children were involved in informal trading, and the mother was largely in charge of this activity. The father was a member of the police force, serving in the special constabulary.[34] He had to supplement his meagre allowance through informal means, such as cobbling. The family also supplemented its earnings by working a small plot to meet its food requirements.

The family lived in an overcrowded area in a police camp, where several families share one block, popularly known as barracks, in a former classroom that is subdivided by curtains and wooden boards to accommodate different families. These family units are further divided into smaller units, which serve as kitchens, bedrooms and lounges. Toilets and bathrooms are shared communally.

Carol's mother sold vegetables at Newlands Shopping Centre. Kumbirai, aged fourteen and the eldest son in the family, was in Form 2 at Harare High School in Mbare. He had to wake up very early to walk about seven kilometres to school, as the parents could not always afford to give him the

---

[34] A special constable is a policeman who helps when there is a crisis or shortage of manpower within the police force, and is paid according to the hours that she or he has worked.

bus fare. However, the mother made an effort to give him money for part of the journey to and from school, so Kumbirai sometimes caught a bus to Mbare in the morning and walked back home after school.

Sometimes, when the mother had no money to buy sufficient vegetables in the morning, Kumbirai had to buy vegetables for his mother from the Mbare market after school. This procedure also ensured that she had fresh vegetables for sale at peak hours when people buy vegetables for evening meals.

He helped his mother at the vegetable stall after school and was left with sole responsibility for it when the mother went home to prepare their supper. Sometimes, when they had closed for the day, he helped his father repair shoes, a chore he did not like because he had to concentrate and do it properly or else father made him undo and redo his stitching. Kumbirai preferred selling vegetables. He said this enabled him to do homework and gave him time to play with friends. Despite this busy schedule, Kumbirai never missed school and actively participated in sports with encouragement from his parents. He was an average performing student and he believed he could do better if had more time to read and go to the library as most of the children did.

His friends used to tease to tease him about his involvement in vending but he did not seem to mind any more because he knew that the family livelihood depends upon it. Kumbirai was, however, protective of his sister Carol, who is three years younger than him. He did not take it lightly when his friends or any other person teased her.

Carol, aged 11, was in Grade 5 at the local Tomlinson Primary School and, like her brother, never missed school. Her duties were mainly confined to the house, not only because she was young, but also because the family believed that the street is no place for a little girl. Given the overcrowded living environment, however, and lack of privacy, there is very little that families can do to keep their children at home. Most children spend their time outside in the streets playing with friends. Carol normally cleaned the house, washed the dishes, and baby-sat her younger sibling. She was still too young to prepare meals for the family. She helped her mother at the vegetable stall, especially when her brother Kumbirai was playing sports. Her mother often left Carol attending the stall under the supervision of the other vendors, when she went to prepare the evening meal or if she had urgently to go somewhere.

Her school had 'hot-seating' sessions,[35] and she sold freezits by the school gate to other school children before she went into class, or after classes when she attended school in the morning. Carol seemed to handle very well the mix between school and work. Within the school setting, Carol's sales did not disrupt her school schedule. Her handling of money made her adept in issuing quick change, which demands a good command of basic numbers. Furthermore, handling money made her well acquainted with money management, and how to determine profits from initial purchase price and other related costs, and on occasion to appreciate losses if she ever encountered them.

Despite all the work that Carol did, both at home and in school, she found time to play and get involved in other activities common among children her age. However, her earning role earned her the nickname '*mafreezit*' from her classmates and teachers.

Carol and Kumbirai could only start doing their homework after they had closed the vegetable stall and eaten their supper.

---

[35] In 'hot seating', where school infrastructure is limited, two groups of children use the same school facilities, with some children attending morning classes and others attending afternoon classes.

This was normally long after seven in the evening, when other children were already preparing for bed. They were often in trouble at school for not finishing their homework. Their mother stated that she would go any length to educate her children. She was, however, more worried about Carol, whom she always encouraged to work even harder, because she wants her to lead a better life. She contended:

> My child, in this day and era you cannot afford to ignore educating your children. If you give them basic education, you will have empowered them to compete at the same level with others on the job market. If they fail to utilise the opportunity, they will not blame me because I will have done my part. I worry about Carol, as a girl. As you can see, I am here by the roadside. A woman's place is no longer in the kitchen, as the woman has to go out and look for the bread and butter before she can come and cook in the kitchen. In these difficult times that we are living in, a woman should never sit on her hands and wait for the husband to provide.

Carol's mother stopped talking for a while, took a deep breath, and continued:

> I want my Carol to have an education so that she can get an office job, or become a nurse. I do not want her to lead the kind of life I am leading. My parents did not send me to school because they thought it was a waste of resources to educate a girl, and I have never forgiven them for that, since my peers who managed to go to school are leading a far much better life than me.

Although the children's mother wished that her children did not have to work, poverty compelled her to use their help.

Photograph by Tsvangirayi Mukwazhi

🐾 What We Have Learned 🐾

Rumbidzai Rurevo and Michael Bourdillon

Why girls are on the streets

Our case studies, like much previous research,[36] indicate that there is no single cause for children to be on the streets, but that they are pushed into their situation by a combination of factors that make life impossible at home. These factors are both societal and individual. Societal factors include economic circumstances, both within the country and internationally, the inferior status of women, and of girls in particular, problems in the education system, and the HIV/AIDS epidemic. Individual factors, such as conflicts with elders or poor performance at school, are specific to the children and their families.

In an ideal family situation in Zimbabwe's cultures, girls are perceived to be temperamentally inclined to stay close to home. They do not rebel against restrictions as much as boys do and are assumed to have higher tolerance levels for bad or abusive treatment.

---

[36] On Harare, see L. Dube, Street Children: a part of organised society? Unpublished D.Phil. Dissertation, University of Zimbabwe, Harare, 1999. See also A. Campbell, *The Girls in the Gang*, Blackwell, Oxford, 1991; A. Chatterjee, *India: The Forgotten children of the cities*, Innocenti studies, UNICEF, 1992.

This stereotype of girls has some foundation, but girls do sometimes resort to the streets when they have tried all other options. Boys on the other hand venture into street life at a much earlier age than girls, and are consequently more numerous there.

Most of our cases are linked to poverty, and the growing number of girls on the streets is an indicator of worsening poverty. Families live on minimal incomes, often eked out in the informal economy, which requires long working hours for small returns, and contributions from all members of the family including children. Some children are on the streets because their parents cannot afford a more stable home.

Growing poverty affects women in particular. Many of the girls that were interviewed had mothers who were struggling to survive and to provide for their children without male help. Only one of the girls had any support from her father – this was our last case, Carol, who was only peripherally on the streets. Many women have to supplement the meagre incomes of their male partners, and some become the principal breadwinners for their families. This has resulted in a rapidly growing informal sector, and, correspondingly, a rise in young people, both boys and girls, participating in the informal economy in a pooling of family labour. At the same time, this informal economy has been the avenue of survival for those children who find themselves on their own, outside the traditional protection of a family.

The poverty of women is exacerbated by the subordinate position of women in Zimbabwean society. In the case of Babra, a woman and her children were hounded out of her home on the death of her husband by the latter's relatives: this is not an uncommon occurrence in the country. A man sometimes feels free to drive a woman from his home when conflicts arise. The common economic dependence of women on men makes women particularly vulnerable.

The appearance of street girls is partly linked to the growth of the informal sector in the face of general decline in the Zimbabwean economy and the ravaging impact of HIV/AIDS. In many cultures, girls are socialised to remain at home so as to preserve their purity and to make them desirable as women and mothers. Nevertheless, some girls are socialised into street life because their mothers are street vendors and marketers and, as young daughters accompany, imitate, and help their mothers, they gain access to life on the streets. In some cases, these girls are sent by their mothers to scavenge for things, to beg and commit petty crime. There is an element of socialisation to work on the streets.

We observed, however, that when children are involved in informal trade on the streets with the support and encouragement of their families – and particularly when they have a home, however meagre, to return to – their work can be constructive and a source of dignity and pride. In the cases of Catherine, Kumbirai and Carol, we found children who coped well with working on the streets to raise money towards the family's rent or to pay school fees for siblings.

A common feature in the cases we have presented is a breakdown in family structures. The children are born without the social sanction of marriage, and the father is unknown or takes no responsibility for the children. Poor people cannot afford the luxury of marriage negotiations and payments. Living from hand to mouth often makes long-term commitments impossible. Although unions are sometimes relatively stable, these are not formal marriages with the commitment for the future that marriage involves. Children born to these unions cannot always call on the support of both parents, which is particularly a problem when the one supporting them dies. While some women manage to care for their children without male support, others fail to cope, and their children are particularly vulnerable.

Violence and abuse within the home is a common concomitant of poverty and lies behind some of our cases. We have seen the case of Cynthia and Catherine where wealth encouraged the father to spend money on drink and women, neglect his daughters and beat his wife.

Sometimes children are supported by extended family. In the current harsh economic climate, however, relatives often resent having an extra mouth to feed. Children in need of support may not be fully welcomed by members of the extended family, and they often suffer various kinds of abuse from them. We have seen cases of kin imposing heavy domestic burdens on children, demanding income from them, even by prostitution, and sometimes sexually abusing them. When the girls complain, they are beaten or driven away, betrayed by the adult world.

Frequently, the break-up of the family structure is associated with HIV/AIDS and the death of a parent. The number of deaths in the close families of the girls we met shows how devastating the HIV/AIDS epidemic is in the lives of children.

Cultural expectations of the roles of girls may occasionally push one out of her home and into a life on the streets. We saw how one girl, Buhle, was sent to do housekeeping chores for an aunt, and felt exploited. Occasionally, girls rebel against the expectation for them to be submissive and work hard within the household, and have only restricted contacts outside the home. Related to this is the failure of some adults to value the education of girl children or to make it a priority.

In several cases, we found children having problems at school. Buhle, for example, expressed little interest in academic work and found no opportunity for developing her other talents. In some instances, the children were not doing particularly well at school. Their situation was not helped by the taunts of other children.

The stigma they acquire is a problem for street children, and a hindrance to returning to family life off the streets. We heard from a girl who was afraid to go home because of what her family would say about this part of her life. We have also seen the case of Shamiso, who was not allowed to return home and was driven back to the streets because cultural marriage norms had not been met. Taunts from other children can send children back onto the streets; stepparents can cite the street life of children as a reason for keeping them out of their home. We have seen and heard how street girls are despised by people they meet.

Coping

A minority of girls on the street seem to be able to earn an income to help their families without incurring evident physical or moral harm. Such girls, we discovered in our study, had a home to go to at night and were supported by their families. They also received help from older women who were trading together with them on the streets.

Once they are living on the streets, it is difficult for girls to survive without help from men. Street girls have fewer opportunities to make a living on the streets than do boys. The girls in this study were limited to petty vending, begging (sometimes using infants to attract sympathy), and sex. Girls are liable to be harassed by officials and by boys and men on the streets. Boys sometimes drive girls away from areas where they are competing in vending. Like older street women,[37] the way for a girl to cope is to have a man to look after her, or perhaps to align herself with a protective gang of boys. Such support comes in exchange for sexual favours.

Sexual services and prostitution are an important source of income for street girls, even as it endangers their lives. Coming onto the streets at a later age than do many boys, girls have often already reached puberty, which means that they are perceived, and often evaluated, in sexual terms. Street girls often beget children by different men, who do not regard them as legitimate wives worthy of receiving financial support.

Another factor that drives girls into sexual activities is the view of many men in our society that they have a right to sex, much as they have the right to food and drink. There is a perception that men

---

[37] See M.F.C. Bourdillon, *Poor, Harassed, But Very Much Alive: An Account of Street People and their Organisation.* Mambo Press, Gweru, 1991: 53.

cannot live complete lives without sex, and so have a right to it in whatever way they can. This attitude becomes particularly dangerous to children when it is associated with a belief that sex with a virgin can cure them of illness (particularly HIV/AIDS) or help them to get rich. The men in the street community appear to feel free to have sex with young girls, sometimes against their will. Businessmen feel free to hire young girls for sex. Even though the law prohibits sex with minors, we live in a society in which the law carries little moral status.

Apart from raising incomes in whatever ways they can, we also found girls manipulating welfare organisations that support street children. They would find ways to adapt their circumstances and their stories to obtain particular services, but resist compromising their independence.

Interventions

Apart from the general desperate situation of street children in Harare, the situation is worse for the younger street boys and street girls, who are marginalised within programmes dominated by the older street boys. Organisations such as Streets Ahead have focused primarily on boys in the activities and facilities they offer to children. There is a need to provide more explicitly for girls. In particular, there is a need to deal directly with sexuality and the reproductive health rights of street girls, who are at high risk of HIV infection and of bearing children without being able to care for them. Any girl on the streets is very vulnerable to sexual abuse and HIV infection. This makes prevention the key intervention, and the removal of young girls from the streets immediately they arrive there.[38]

---

[38] Since this research was undertaken, Streets Ahead has been paying attention to girls. Also it has been paying more attention to reuniting children with their families before they get established in street life.

But it is not clear what form such intervention should take, nor what intervention is appropriate for girls who have been on the streets for some time and are already HIV positive. Restrictive programmes that compel girls to enter homes and institutions have not been very successful. The girls resent such compulsion and the loss of their freedom. They also resent the lack of dignity with which they are usually treated. When rounded up and placed in institutions, they regularly abscond. Procedures that do not respect them are unlikely to achieve anything that benefits the girls.

The failure of many programmes for street children is due to the tendency to try to rescue them from street life without providing realistic alternatives. If children are fleeing abuse and an intolerable situation at home, it does not help to make them return to the same home and the same conditions. Many programmes do not teach the street children how to survive in the world beyond the streets.[39] This study suggests the futility of simply trying to remove children from the streets. In certain circumstances, given what is possible, the streets may provide the most viable form of livelihood for some of them. Food and income at least keeps them alive in the short term. Arresting street children for begging, scavenging, or stealing, then placing them in approved institutions, will not improve the circumstances that pushed them onto the streets in the first place. It is sometimes argued that such interventions are based on western, or middle-class, notions of childhood, in which children are regarded as incompetent and in need of control as well as care.

Successful interventions need, therefore, to appreciate the problems as experienced by the children themselves, to respect their competence and their right to take part in making decisions that affect their lives. On the other hand, our cases show the difficulty

---

[39] See Swart, J. 'Street children in Latin America with special reference to Guatemala', *Unisa Latin America Report* 6 (1) March 1990: 37. Also L. Aptekar, 'Street Children in Nairobi, Kenya: Gender Differences and Mental Health,' paper presented at the African Regional ISSBD Workshop, Lusaka Zambia, 1996.

that girls have in adapting to a more disciplined life after tasting the freedom of the streets. It appears inevitable that girls on the streets will take up sexual practices that are harmful to themselves and to the children they bear – particularly in the context of HIV/AIDS. Their right to such freedom is questionable.

One approach is to try to empower the children with knowledge and skills. Included in this approach is education about their rights, and particularly about the rights of children. Such knowledge, however, is not helpful when children are not able to demand these rights and others are not able or willing to defend them.

There have been programmes to provide street children with knowledge of AIDS, which have had limited success. The girls in our study were no different from other street children, who generally know that AIDS is not curable and that it is transmitted through sex. Like many in adult society, however, they do not understand the long dormant residence of the virus in the body, and think that sex with someone who appears healthy is relatively safe.[40] Besides, street children are at an age in which danger is often ignored in the face of immediate experiences. Their general circumstances make them unlikely to think much about the remote future. It is not enough to provide education about health and rights, without offering new opportunities for a better life.

Girls need knowledge and skills that will enable them to earn and survive in less harmful ways. This is the more significant form of empowerment than education. Training in general and specific income-generating skills might help. It is difficult, however, for disadvantaged children to earn their keep in a climate of economic collapse and severe poverty. In Zimbabwe today, there is heavy competition for any source of income. Children are further

---

[40] See L.Dube, 'Aids-Risk Patterns and Knowledge of the Disease Amongst Street Children in Harare, Zimbabwe.' *Journal of Social Development in Africa* 12 (1997), 2: 70-72. On street children in South Africa see Linda M. Richter and Jill Swart-Kruger, 'AIDS-risk among street children and youth: implications for intervention', *South African Journal of Psychology*, 25 (1995), 1, 31-38.

disadvantaged by an attitude that refuses to recognise their economic activities, which makes their employment illegal and makes them dangerously vulnerable to exploitation: a campaign against child labour does not help street children. Protected employment for desperate children could help them.

Another form of empowerment is to involve the children in making decisions that affect their lives, which is not only their right but is also likely to gain their greater co-operation in programmes. In Brazil, a National Movement of Street Children was formed, in line with movements for working children. Involving the children in the programmes that would improve their lives had some effect.[41] There have been attempts to involve the children in Harare, but these have had limited scope and success. It may help to bring the children into the planning of the programmes, rather than involving them only at the stage of implementation. Staff of Streets Ahead work and consult with older street children, or 'street peers', who represent the needs of the children, and through this approach the organisation has managed to help some of the girls. Streets Ahead and Girl Child Network organise workshops where children are the main participants. But improvement in the lives of the girls is sometimes only temporary, and these organisations have not on the whole succeeded in preventing girls from engaging in activities that are likely to result in HIV/AIDS and child pregnancies. Infected girls readily pass on the HIV to their friends among the boys.

Some success has come from the system of employing older street children to care for younger children, and particularly to bring children newly on the streets to the attention of staff of the intervening organisation. Nevertheless, the street peers are children who successfully provide for themselves on the streets, in a street

---

[41] See Anthony Swift, *Children for social change; education for citizenship of street children and working children in Brazil.* Educational Heretics Press, Nottingham, 1997.

culture of exploiting and being exploited. Their work needs careful guidance and monitoring. Some children have alleged that street peers on occasion delay passing on the information for a few days while they make a little money out of the naïve children newly on the streets. The peers concerned deny the charges, which could well arise from jealousy because of the stipend that the peers receive. Whether or not they are true, the allegations illustrate the problems involved in giving responsibility to children who have learned to survive on the streets.

What can be done to help?

For a few girls the streets provide a means of livelihood, enable them to support themselves and their families, and at the same time to acquire self-esteem. Success in that environment seems possible only with a supportive network, particularly within their families, however impoverished. Perhaps one appropriate form of intervention is to provide a supportive network for working children. Instead of harassing them and making their work illegal, authorities should support opportunities for the children to earn an income, safely and under conditions that can be monitored.

For most street girls the situation is desperate. They have very limited sources of sustenance, and no proper accommodation or regular, healthy food. They are deprived of education and are at high risk of HIV infection. Many have babies when they are too young, and lack the basic means, to care for them. Others find ways to abort their pregnancies, which are often dangerous to the health of the girls. They are dependent on boys and men who cannot be relied upon to treat them well, even if they had the means to do so. They are subject to harassment from other street people, from the public, and from officials. For street girls, then, living on the streets is not only risky and rough, but can also be humiliating and dehumanising as one tries to survive. But once they have tasted the freedom and independence of the streets, and a quick income from sex, it is hard for them to adapt to any other kind of life.

Nevertheless, this study calls into question an approach that accepts the decisions of children to come onto the streets as a solution to worse problems elsewhere, and which point to the resilience of children and their coping mechanisms to weigh against their vulnerability.[42] In the current situation, life on the streets means a high probability of HIV infection and death from AIDS. Outreach work is essential to identify potential street children as soon as they come onto the streets, with the aim of finding alternatives for them.

Once they are established on the streets, the girls are difficult to help. The minimum that adults can do is to provide an environment, including an educational environment that respects their persons, and provides services to improve the short life that remains for them.

Perhaps the main conclusion of this study is support for the popular perception that the streets are not a good place for girls. The girls know this, but such a stance is unhelpful unless adults can provide them with viable alternatives. And alternatives will not be viable if they do not respect the girls as individuals.

Most people in society can do little to help these girls. Even organisations dedicated to helping desperate children find it hard to provide street girls with a life that can be lived with dignity. From among the many interventions possible, however, the findings of our study highlight a few that can offer genuine, if limited, hope. They include:

➢ Those children who are managing to cope on the streets need a support network, to protect them from abuse and to provide guidance for their activities. Such support requires adults with the time and willingness to treat each child as an individual person, and to attend to the child's specific situation. Instead

---

[42] See for example M.F.C. Bourdillon, 'Street children in Harare': 529. For a good discussion of this issue, see David Donald and Jill Swart-Kruger, 'The South African street child: developmental implications,' *South African Journal of Psychology*, 24 (1994), 4, 169-174.

of harassment and laws that criminalise their work. Street children can benefit from opportunities to earn an income, safely and under conditions that can be monitored.

> There is urgent need for more welfare for street children. While the welfare services of the state are over-stretched, there have been moves to improve the situation of children through, for instance, the AIDS levy and through work on a child-friendly budget. Non-governmental organisations trying to help need both practical and financial support. Nevertheless, numbers are such that it is unlikely that all street children can be adequately provided for in the foreseeable future.

> Outreach work is essential to identify potential street children as soon as they come onto the streets, with the aim of finding alternatives for them.

> Profound changes in society's attitudes. Destructive attitudes and priorities lie behind the plight of some of the girls in this study. Here are some of the areas where change is needed.

  • Poor people should receive sympathy and respect rather than vilification. We have seen problems created for the girls by the attitudes of other school children, officials, and society at large. It is hard, however, to respect the poor in a society in which status and success are closely identified with material wealth. In the current economic climate, we need to understand, and make sure our children understand, that many people are destitute through no fault of their own.

  • Street girls need acceptance rather than rejection. When a girl drops out from the normal life of children, moral outrage by kin and others, and insistence on cultural practices, can hinder her rehabilitation. People responsible for the girls need to be flexible and find ways of asserting their values without rejecting the girls.

- The subordinate position of women still needs urgently to be addressed. Lack of security in marriage (particularly on the death of the husband) and in the home can eventually drive girls onto the streets. Inequalities in earning power also causes suffering. Girls are further discriminated against when their education is not seen as important.

- An assumption that men have a right to sex needs to be opposed rigorously.

- All sex with minors needs to become socially unacceptable, to support the law which clearly prohibits such practices.

- Children need an environment in which they can have confidence in the authorities. They need to know with certainty that those in authority will listen with respect to their appeals for help. They must also have confidence that those in authority will never connive with people who exploit children in any way.

➢ Children who find it hard to leave the streets, and who are probably in any case infected by HIV, need services to enable them to live with some dignity and without infecting others. They need facilities for washing and food preparation, and to be able to relax and play. They need treatment when they are hurt or ill. They need education that treats them with respect. They need people who will listen to them with respect and understanding and who will give them some hope in a society that has treated them so badly.

Photograph courtesy of Streets Ahead

Girl taking time out at the Streets Ahead drop-in centre (see p. 11)

ぞ 64 ぞ

🐒 Bibliography 🐒

Agnelli, S 1986 *Street Children: A Growing Urban Tragedy*. Weidenfeld and Nicholson, London.

Aptekar, L. 1994 'Street Children in the Developing World: A Review of their Condition' in *Cross Cultural Research* 28, 3: 195-224.

Aptekar, L. 1996 'Street Children in Nairobi, Kenya: Gender Differences and Mental Health.' A paper presented at the African Regional ISSBD Workshop, Lusaka Zambia.

Baker, R. 1998 'Runaway Street Children in Nepal: Social Competence Away from Home' in *Children and Social Competence: Areas of Action* (ed.) Ian Hutchby and Jo Moran-Ellis. Falmer Press, London: 46-63.

Bourdillon, M.F.C. 1991 *Poor, Harassed, But Very Much Alive: An Account of Street People and their Organisation*. Mambo Press, Gweru.

Bourdillon, M.F.C. 1994 'Street children in Harare'. *Africa* 64, 4: 516-32.

Bourdillon, M.F.C. 1997 *Where are the Ancestors? Changing Culture in Zimbabwe*. University of Zimbabwe Press (2nd ed.), Harare.

Bourdillon, M.F.C. 2000 *Earning a Life: Working Children in Zimbabwe*. Weaver Press, Harare.

Butcher, A. 1996 *Street Children*. Nelson Word Publishing, Nashville.

Butler, U. and I. Rizzini, 2001 'Young people living and working on the streets of Brazil: revisiting the literature', *International Journal of Educational Policy, Research and Practice* (University of South Florida, USA), 2 , 4.

Campbell, A. 1991 *The Girls in the Gang*. Blackwell, Oxford.

Chatterjee, A. 1992 India: The Forgotten children of the cities. *Innocenti studies*. UNICEF

Chirwa, Y. and Wakatama, M. 2000 'Working Street Children in Harare' in *Earninga Life: working children in Zimbabwe* (ed) Bourdillon, M.F.C. 2000. Weaver Press, Harare.

Donald, David, and Jill Swart-Kruger, 1994, 'The South African street child: developmental implications,' *South African Journal of Psychology*, 24, 4, 169-74.

Dube, L. 1997 'Aids-Risk Patterns and Knowledge of the Disease Amongst Street Children in Harare, Zimbabwe.' *Journal of Social Development in Africa* 12, 2: 61-73.

Dube, L. 1999 *Street Children: a part of organised society?* Unpublished D.Phil. Dissertation, University of Zimbabwe, Harare.

Dube, L., Kamvura, L., and Bourdillon, M.F.C. 1996 'Working with street boys in Harare.' *Africa Insight* 26, 3: 260-67.

Ennew, J. 1994 *Street and working children: A guide to planning*. Save the Children, London.

Felsman, J.K. 1984 'Abandoned children: a reconsideration.' *Children Today*. May-June 1984.

Glauser, B. 1990 'Street Children: Deconstructing a Construct'. In *Constructing and Reconstructing Childhood: Contemporary Issues in the Sociological Study of Childhood* (ed.) A. James and A. Prout. Falmer Press: London. 136-56.

Grier, B. 1996 'Street kids in Zimbabwe: The historical origins of a contemporary problem,' a paper presented at the Annual Meeting of the African Studies Association, November 25, 1996 San Fransisco, CA, USA.

Lopi, B. and Kiremire, M.K. 2001 *Invisible Girls: The Life Circumstances and Legal Situation of Street Girls in Lusaka*. Zambia Association for Research and Development and Movement of Community Action for the Prevention and Protection of Young People Against Poverty, Destitution, Diseases and Exploitation, Lusaka.

Mapedzahama, V. and Bourdillon, M.F.C. 2000 'Street workers in a Harare suburb' in *Earning a Life: Working children in Zimbabwe* (ed.) Bourdillon, M.F.C. 2000, Weaver Press, Harare.

Muchini, B. and Nyandiya - Bundy, S 1991 'Struggling to survive; study of Street Children in Zimbabwe'. Department of Psychology, University of Zimbabwe, and UNICEF, Harare.

Mutisi, M. and Bourdillon, M.F.C. 2000 'Child vendors at a rural growth point'. In *Earning a Life: Working children in Zimbabwe* (ed.) Michael Bourdillon. Weaver Press, Harare, 75-94.

Myers, W.E. and Boyden, J. 1998 *Child labour: Promoting the best interests of working children*. Save the Children(UK), London.

Richter, Linda M. and Jill Swart-Kruger, 1995, 'AIDS-risk among street children and youth: implications for intervention'. *South African Journal of Psychology*, 25, 1, 31-38.

Save the Children 2000 *Directory of Children's Services in Zimbabwe – 2000*. Save the Children (UK), Harare

Swart-Kruger, J. 1996 'An imperfect fit – street children and state intervention'. *Africa Insight* 26, 3: 231-35.

Swart , J. 1988 *An anthropological study of street children in Hillbrow Johannesburg, with special reference to their moral values*. M.A.Thesis in Anthropology, University of South Africa.

Swart, J. 1990 'Street children in Latin America with special reference to Guatemala'. *Unisa Latin America Report* (Pretoria) 6 (1). March 1990: 28-42.

Swift, A. 1997 *Children for Social Change: Education for citizenship of street children and working children in Brazil.* Educational Heretics Press, Nottingham.

UNICEF 1999 *Zimbabwe Progress Report.* Harare.

Vitachi, A. 1989 *Stolen childhood: In search of the rights of the child.* Polity Press, Cambridge.

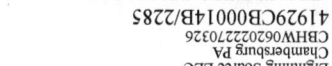